Tears of Poignancy

Twenty years of poetry
from the pen of Essex author

Ian Yearsley

Published by Ian Yearsley

Publishing partner: Paragon Publishing, Rothersthorpe

First published 2006

© Ian Yearsley 2006

The rights of Ian Yearsley to be identified as the author of this work have been asserted by him in accordance with the Copyright, Designs and Patents Act of 1988.

All rights reserved; no part of this publication may be reproduced, stored in a retrieval system, or transmitted in any form or by any means, electronic, mechanical, photocopying, recording or otherwise without the prior written consent of the publishers or a licence permitting copying in the UK issued by the Copyright Licensing Agency Ltd, 90 Tottenham Court Road, London W1P 9HE.

ISBN 1-899820-22-1 Paperback

Book design, layout and production management by Into Print

www.intoprint.net

Printed and bound in UK and USA by Lightning Source

Author contact:

Ian Yearsley, P.O. Box 5360, Westcliff-on-Sea, Essex, SS0 9FF

Contents

1. Cockles at Leigh
2. Sonnet
3. She hardly says a word, she is so shy...
4. They've passed us by, those happy times...
5. Commuting from Leigh
6. Dedham Vale
7. Counsel for the Defence (The Teachers' Song)
8. Perfection
9. In Pursuit of Success
10. It may just be a passing glance...
11. Owners of the World
12. Death on the Rock and in Other Places
13. There is no point, my Lord, in all of this...
14. Happy New Year (3)
15. Prelude to the Battle of Ashingdon (1016): The English Camp
16. Life Sonnet
17. Chasing Tails
18. The Essex Marshlands
19. The Visitors' Book at St Mary's
20. Discipline, Not Timing
21. Dedham
22. Love's Deft Embrace
23. Dream Girl
24. It Changed My Life
25. Lament for Thirtysomethings
26. At Writtle, in August
27. Essex
28. In Fryerning Churchyard
29. Prelude to the Battle of Ashingdon (1016): The Danish Camp
30. Stop Pretending

About the Author

Ian Yearsley was born in 1965 in Ingatestone, Essex and currently lives in Eastwood, Essex, about 15 miles to the south-east of his native village. He is well-known for his interest in his home county and has written a number of books on the subject, including The Islands of Essex, Essex Events, A History of Southend, Hadleigh Past, Rayleigh: A History, Ingatestone & Fryerning: A History and Dedham, Flatford & East Bergholt: A Pictorial History. Several of these have topped local bestseller lists. He has also written on the subject of researching local history, has led local history writing workshops and has taken part in various radio documentaries about Essex places.

Throughout the 1990s Ian was a regular contributor to magazines like Essex Countryside, This Month in Essex and Essex Ghosts & Hauntings and he is, or has been, a member of various county heritage and environmental groups, such as the Essex Mills Group, the Friends of Essex Churches and the Essex Wildlife Trust. He has led or been involved in several local environmental and heritage campaigns, including one which led to the creation of the popular Cherry Orchard Jubilee Country Park on the borders of Southend and Rochford. He has also written on a wide range of subjects for a number of national and regional magazines.

In the early 1990s two of Ian's poems, The Essex Marshlands and Prelude to the Battle of Ashingdon (1016): The English Camp, were published in national poetry anthologies and in 1997 Southend Library hosted an exhibition featuring 17 of Ian's poems on a variety of subjects. Such was the interest amongst exhibition visitors, and amongst attendees of a poetry workshop that he led three years later, that Ian has been persuaded to take a break from local history writing and publish a collection of his poems. The result is this selection of 30 poems, which has been produced in time to commemorate his 20th anniversary as a published writer.

The poems in this collection cover a 22-year period from 1984 to 2006, the later poems showing Ian's increasing maturity and development as a writer. Much of Ian's poetry examines the concept of despair. The themes of thwarted ambition, disappointment in Love and disillusionment with Life run through it like a thread through cloth. By no means all of his work is pessimistic, however. His positive Essex poems (including the two mentioned above) and his bright humorous works complement well the sadness which overwhelms the poems of Life and Love. Examples covering all these subjects are featured in this collection.

Apart from his best-selling books, Ian has also won several awards for his writing, including an Originality Award for his first book, The Islands of Essex, and a Twist-in-the-Tail Award for his short story, The Fungus from Outer Space. He has also been a winner in an Essex photographic competition and he co-wrote the music to an award-winning amateur film.

More information about Ian's work can be found on his website at http://myweb.tiscali.co.uk/ianyearsley

Cockles at Leigh

Shrouded church towers over Leigh,
Bells hail a dawn I cannot see,
Boats sail from mist with tourists' tea,
Expose tradition's haul to me.

Behind me, church towers over all,
From inland Leigh to new seawall,
From church to sea does History sprawl
As Osborne's greets the day's first haul.

I cross the lines that split the town
(On Leigh's first trains the townsfolk frowned)
As for the cockle sheds I'm bound:
I'm glad to say they're still around.

Though early, work is in full flow:
The shellfish is prepared for show,
'The customer is right, you know,'
Though blind to toil the cocklers know.

Surprised that groups protect Old Leigh:
Church, cocklers, cobbles, boats and sea?
Appreciate this place like me
For it is steeped in History

And this day's mist adds mystery.

(1984)

Sonnet

Do not despise me for my leaving you,
When finally you've calmed and stepping back
You've thought my act a selfish thing to do
Since taking time to set me on the track.

And over my departure do not grieve
Nor hold yourself responsible for me.
It's nothing that you did which made me leave
I hope my explanations help you see:

For years I've thought our time is being wasted,
That golden key I'd found could not make mine.
Sweet flavour savoured, why want others tasted?
Like water when compared with sweetest wine.

I have no key to get me through above:
Despite persistence, could not win her love.

(1984)

She hardly says a word, she is so shy...

She hardly says a word, she is so shy.
She's difficult to talk to at the start.
Such blushing silence wouldn't hurt a fly!
Such innocence and purity of heart.

Yet once she is at ease, the eyes tell all --
Alluring look no suitor can resist --
Recounting tales of when she had a ball,
Each treasured inch of body warmly kissed.

To all she seems so innocent and pure,
Until one gets to know her wicked ways:
No longer is she charming and demure --
There's 'double-entendre' in everything she says.

It's funny how we witness such a change,
Yet tragedy that one should act so strange.

(1984)

They've passed us by, those happy times...

They've passed us by, those happy times, gone now,
And they are out of reach of even I
And it is oh so hard to fathom how
To capture that which once had ruled our sky.

The chance to make or break has come to this
And what hope is there but to write and die?
The search for fame still ranks above a kiss:
Such irony, as she is standing by.

Keep writing, for the words will always come
That are to make an impact on the world;
No phrase affect so many as the one
Which once in torment kept its author curled.

So, never let the pen from paper rise
'Til the candle no more flickers in the eyes.

(1986)

Commuting from Leigh

The beauty of the crisp early morning's brisk stroll is eroded
In that long descent from the seventh Heaven
Where I can see the world
To the 7:36 which will whisk me to its centre,
As every inch draws me closer to the City,
Takes me further from this Eden.

The friendly tinkle of the yachts at their moorings
And the gentle lapping
Of the sun-soaked sea on the cockle-shell shore
Is left behind me.

The constant clickety-clack carries me
Past Benfleet's bloodied battlefields
Where yesterday wars were won and lost
In Sunday soccer confrontations.

The rising emerald tide of traffic lights grows greener,
Signalling the City that approaches.

Not until the evening will peace be mine again,
When that same hill which once was as a foe
Will lead the way to Heaven as a friend.

(1987)

Dedham Vale

John Constable was born perhaps a mile away
From the very spot we're standing now.
Two centuries ago he painted landscapes here
While his father's land was under plough.

See this picture of a waggon in a river here,
With a little cottage on the bank?
You can see it over there, it hasn't changed at all,
And look here's where the horses drank.

Flatford Mill was one of John's favourite haunts
And the little wooden bridge still remains.
Across the meadow you can see the tower of Dedham church:
Nothing in this place has changed.

The charming church in Bergholt's but a hundred yards
From the site of where his birthplace stood.
You can recognise the strong stone structure from his work
And the separate bell-tower crafted in wood.

Though popular with people John was never praised
By his critics, who were many and loud,
But of reaching all the goals he always sought to attain
The artist was deservedly proud.

He finally achieved the status he'd long sought --
Showed Suffolk scenes as JC RA --
And froze in Time the countryside of Dedham Vale
Which, thank God, retains its beauty today.

(1987)

Counsel for the Defence
(The Teachers' Song)

There's a fault in our social structure:
It begins at the gates to the school
Where the children are dumped by their parents,
Who go home to sip Pimms by the pool.

So it's left up to us to instruct them
In ways of the world, make them good,
Give them qualifications and knowledge -
'Cause if we didn't, no-one else would.

Nowhere else would they learn about fitness,
Discipline, sex education -
Their parents disown them and leave them
With us to prepare for the nation.

Yet we're criticised, constantly barracked,
By all - and it's grossly unfair
'Cause we're burdened with shaping the future
And there may come a day WE don't care.

(1987)

Perfection

To seek Perfection ever was Man's aim,
Yet such pursuit was always doomed to fail,
For never is reality the same
As joy that one desires to end the tale.

The shortness of our stay here hinders plans
Which otherwise would reap such rich rewards
And there are none so unfulfilled as Man's
(No other species time to goals affords),

For there is none but Man desires more
And more of all that he's at present got
And every other creature, it is sure,
Is quite contented to endure his lot.

To seek Perfection ever was Man's aim;
Perfection, though, exists in only name.

(1988)

In Pursuit of Success

If only I could make myself believe
That there's no need at all for me to prove
Myself to others who do nothing but perceive
An egotist whose dreams are on the move,

That really I'm a star in my own right
And don't need Stardom's elevating hand,
That I'm a better person than I might
Be when a star, a better chance I'd stand!

Though looking after Number One is worthy
Of commendation, chasing sweet success
Is selfish in the eyes of men more earthly,
Who humbly set their sights on something less.

The choice is as it's always been:
To settle, or pursue a fervent dream?

(1988)

It may just be a passing glance...

It may just be a passing glance,
A whiff of Spring's enamoured fragrance,
Discovery, ecstasy, carnal desire
Or pounding heart, eternal fire,
The taste of joy at something new...
Is this is what's brought me close to you?

It may just be another plane
That beating hearts cannot explain,
A mystic place where two are one,
Where thoughts entwine and passions run.
Here lies purity, and evil too...
Is this what's brought me close to you?

(1988)

Owners of the World

Though owner of the Universe, I knew
But little of its practical potential
And so I thought it wise to try a few
Experiments - for knowledge is essential.
For one of my experiments, now rife,
I used a little planet, known as "Earth" -
I planned to try to cultivate some life,
Believing it would one day prove its worth.
You understand, of course, I must state now,
That scientific research was my aim:
I sought merely to learn things and not how
To rape the world for my commercial gain.
I set to work upon my master plan:
In seven days I had created Man.

Unlike experiments on Earth before,
This one involved a species with a mind,
Intelligence, respect for civil law
And love, so it would never be unkind.
I watched it grow for centuries at first -
I nurtured it until it was full-grown -
Exploited all its innocence and worse
'Til I could trust it to be left alone.
My project was a joy right from its birth -
I watched my species cautiously explore
The wonders of that beautiful place, Earth,
And, having seen them, search for still yet more.

There was no happier scientist than I,
Whose plan evolved as planned as Time went by.

So Man was left alone to prove his worth
(My ventures elsewhere had to be inspected),
Until at length I came back down to Earth
And met with something wholly unexpected.
Though I had been away so short a time
Yet I was horror-struck at what I found,
For in my absence crime had followed crime
And all the good I'd done had been unwound.
Not only was Man warring with himself -
A senseless and a sinful occupation -
He'd turned his growing greed upon all else:
A totally intolerable situation.
Incredulous and angry all in one,
I knew that something big had to be done.

For there was Man, the fruit of my creation,
Exploiting all the beauties of my Earth -
A creature of my own imagination
That I had thought would one day prove its worth -
Chopping down the forests on my planet,
Paving all my countryside with stone,
Extracting all the minerals from my granite
And damming rivers that he did not own.
Toxic waste poured out into my seas,
Man hunted lower life-forms as a sport,
Had no respect for animals or trees,

Appointing himself owner of the lot.
Once green and pleasant land had turned dull grey:
For this destruction, someone had to pay.

On Judgement Day, Man worked hard at his case.
"You understand," he said, "that what I do
Is scientific research of the place.
I've no commercial motive - that's untrue!
It's just a few experiments - no more -
To learn a little of our Earth's potential.
We simply thought it prudent to explore
It all - for knowledge is essential."
Where had I heard those plaintive cries before?
Whose earlier defence had been the same?
But now, through Man, I'd learned Life's foremost law -
That owning other lives was not a game.
I'd studied Life and loved it - that I knew;
Now hating it, I'd have to end it too.

A scientist hates failure and that's why
He looks for different answers when he's wrong,
Rejuvenates failed tests for one last try
At proving that he'd been right all along.
As limitless as Time had seemed to Man,
I knew it spanned one short experiment
And worthlessness of such a venture can
Be to that venture's lasting detriment.
Be warned then, those who think themselves the owners

Of natural wonders that are not their own,
For leaving the concern to generous donors
Ensures your card is marked when Time is done.
Take care to safeguard others' lives, my dears,
For this prolongs their futures and your years.

(1990)

Death on the Rock and in Other Places

It's time to plant another bomb inside the next poor victim's car:

He could survive if we guess wrong, but he won't walk very far.

There'll be, of course, the usual fuss that follows such foul deeds,

But three weeks on the Press soon drop old news that no-one reads

And we can return to our plots and plans in the twilight world we share

With soldiers guarding urban streets and civilians in despair

Where it's only January the First and the New Year's just begun

And we're three lives up on last year's count, while our own losses are none.

Now when we kill we expect our deed to be denounced and shamed,

For we've taken a life and a widowed wife is paralysed or maimed,

But we cannot lose, whatever we do, for if our man is killed

By a soldier seeking justice for his brethren's blood spilled,

That wonderful thing, Hypocrisy, soon raises its beautiful head
And the British forgive any crime once its perpetrator's dead
And a man who kills another man who sought victims to maim
Is by eyes that normally idolize now viewed with an equal shame.

Of course, us cowards are evil men and we care not who we kill
(Though making a subtle political point takes a huge degree of skill),
But retaliation holds no fear for men outside the law:
Brave soldiers who shoot guilty men have paid the price before.

Until there is a change of heart, no justice will be done -
To care when a coward meets his match means the war is never won -
And until the British citizen steps free from this self-deceit,
The semtex and the ticking clock will always mean defeat.

(1990)

There is no point, my Lord, in all of this...

There is no point, my Lord, in all of this,
So why pursue this senseless, futile course,
Expect us to pay homage, show remorse
For having doubts when told this would be bliss?

To you, it's an experiment -- a game
Whose rules are known to none of those who play,
Are cared for by them less in much the way
That you care who it is who takes the blame.

You don't believe that we can hate it here,
Receive complaints as if you didn't care,
For guiltiness in Gods is very rare,
Unlike their tendency to interfere.

Next time you make a world, consider well
And shape it like a Heaven not a Hell.

(1990)

Happy New Year (3)

I always reach this point believing Change
Is round the corner, Life's to start anew,
Yet, though I try my best in all I do,
I never make advancements, which is strange.

The hopefulness there seems to be each year,
The promise of a life a little lighter,
A future striding on and building brighter,
Are simply self-delusions, insincere.

Perhaps one year when I have expectations
Above my station (as I always do)
One of them at last might dare come true
And others share my faith and aspirations.

'Til then, my New Year dreams remain but thus -
One wonders why I each year make a fuss!

(1990)

Prelude to the Battle of Ashingdon (1016): The English Camp

The sunrise seared his eyes and made him squint:
The distant stirrings on Canewdon Hill
Told Edmund peace would not prevail until
The clammy clay had gained a crimson tint.

The night had veiled the vista from his view:
He knew Canute could not be caught 'til dawn,
Was eagerly expectant for the morn,
With which would come the victory for the few.

The swordsman at his side surveyed the scene:
The rising sun bathed both sides in its light.
'The soldiers are prepared, sir, for the fight.'
The brusque response was clipped and clear and clean:

'The Dane dwells on our land, which must be freed.
Advance and teach him what becomes of greed.'

(1991)

Life Sonnet

The thrill of knowing you'd be there each day
When I awoke to face the trials of Life --
The pains of work that cut me like a knife --
Would always ease the debt I had to pay.

My life seemed so much brighter with you there:
To know that you were somewhere close at hand --
Could soften any blows that Hell might land --
Enabled me to face it free from care.

Yet, curiously, the help that saw me through
Was like the flickering shadows in a beam --
Imagine what it's like to have a dream
And know that it will never dare come true.

Without you here the pain is sure to grow:
The void you leave will never let me go.

(1992)

Chasing Tails
(written in the style of *The Iliad*)

As cats attempt to catch contorted tails
Attached to torsos totally their own
And circle ceaseless, senseless, flapping flails
With mits that miss their mark and make them moan

And gloating God is glad and grins with glee
At how His power frustrates the felines' aims
And causes them to seem to you and me
Mere foolish failures, soft, with silly names,

To witnesses a tragi-comic sight
That makes us laugh aloud although a shame
To those that seek success with all their might
But never know success except by name,

So Life itself, for all its planned success,
Ends simply as a study in pointlessness.

(1992)

The Essex Marshlands

'There's nothing here. Why bring me to a place
That's barren, empty, desolate and dead,
A lifeless land that fills one's soul with dread,
An endless prairie wilderness of space?
I've seldom seen such greyness in a sky
Or felt such isolation or despair;
The wind tears through my heart and warns: "Beware!"
And circling, screeching birds give their reply.
The smell of salt says "Retch!" when I inhale.
The odious air asks: "Wretch, why are you here?".
This cheerless, treeless, marshland atmosphere
Conceals all horizons with its veil.
I cannot wait while you just stand and stare -
You'll find me taking brandy at *The Bear*.'

There's nothing here? He does not know this place.
This haunting, daunting fascinating land
Implores receptive hearts to understand
The beauty of its emptiness and space.
The dancing, sparkling sunlight shares the sky
With livid hues of blue and slate and grey;
The wind blows tears of poignancy my way
And wheeling shank and curlew softly cry.
I feel my life refresh when I inhale
And taste the salty freshness of the sea -

There's no-one now for miles around but me
To witness Nature taking off her veil.
You're welcome, friend, to any world you share
With those who look but cannot see what's there.

(1993)

The Visitors' Book at St Mary's

Disturbed by gentle breaths and backhand strokes,
A decade's dust, exposed to fresh new drafts,
Began to dance in stained glass sunlit shafts
And play around the Medieval oaks.

I turned the pages - yellowed, faded, dead -
And sought my name, my words, your epitaph,
My church's story's closing paragraph:
'Goodbye old friend,' the sentence simply said.

Ten years now you've been waiting, empty, still,
And every day that's passed I've prayed for you,
That though redundant you'd find work anew,
As I might in your pulpit, with God's will.

Is this how ancient outcasts correspond?
I'll sign again and reaffirm our bond.

(1994)

Discipline, Not Timing

I gave up smoking last year, in the spring,
Which led to a job offer in July,
A new career in August - just the thing
To finance autumn weekends at Versailles.

'A funny time to give up!' friends had mocked.
'It's not the New Year now, you know,' they'd jeered.
'There's no time like the present.' They looked shocked.
'Why wait 'til then and fail like you?' I sneered.

'We gave up smoking New Year! Drinking, too!
And swearing, lying, cheating, being rude...'
'And when d'you start again?' The air turned blue.
'Mid-January some time,' they said, subdued.

'I'll do it my way, thanks, and start today.
Self-discipline, not timing, that's the way!'

(1994)

Dedham

Dedham High Street, open aspect,
Full of tourists, short on space,
Towering church, St Mary's grandeur,
Built by merchants - cloth and lace.
An artist came here, saw and painted,
Captured people long-since dead;
Same but different, something missing,
Decades passing through my head...

...Back to 18th-century Dedham -
Constable came here to school,
Across the fields from distant Bergholt,
Birthplace and most precious jewel
Within the painter's own surroundings,
Loved like none beyond the pale,
Within the mental fence erected,
Cherished scenes of Dedham Vale.

Now on walls throughout the Kingdom
Works of art by artists hang,
In living rooms from Kent to Shetland
Voices have for centuries sang
The praises of the greatest landscape
Painter that there's ever been -
John Constable of Bergholt, Suffolk,
Who captured native Suffolk scenes.

(1995)

Love's Deft Embrace

I always thought I knew Love's deft embrace:
The pleasure and the pain she carried round.
I'd pushed her to the limit and had found
Extremes of joy and heartache in one place.

I'd tasted pleasures some would never know:
Held Ecstasy in her most warm embrace.
Or so I thought until I saw your face
And realised there was higher still to go.

I'd seen Despair through tears of searing pain:
The bitterest tears that one could ever view.
At least I thought they were until I knew
Your path and mine must separate again.

I always thought I knew Love's deft embrace,
But never did until I saw your face.

(1995)

Dream Girl

I must not think of you throughout the day
Must not let my heart jump when you appear
I must avert my eyes when you draw near
Must not show signs of love in any way

Must not let my lips kiss you when you're here
Must not reach out for you when you pass by
Must not be there to hold you when you cry
Must not let my emotions interfere

Must choose my words with care in what I say
Must keep relations formal and sincere
Must hide the truth behind some fake veneer
Must never touch the wonders I survey

But in my dreams, when God comes from above,
You're mine to hold, to cherish and to love.

(1996)

It Changed My Life

It changed my life the day I saw your face.
I'd heard of Love but not felt her embrace,
Had always laughed at others when they'd said
She'd one day rule my life, my heart, my head;
With nothing else I knew was that the case.

Then I met you. My pulse began to race,
My heart did something strange I could not place.
From that first glance my scepticism fled.
It changed my life.

So this was Love. A touch as light as lace,
A Goddess whom I worshipped for her grace,
Who ruled my life, possessed my heart and head,
Until the day came that I knew I'd dread:
Where you once were there was an empty space.
It changed my life.

(1996)

Lament for Thirtysomethings
(Dedicated to Philip Larkin)

It's all a fucking total waste of time!
You live. You die. You wonder why.
Who knows?
Who fucking cares?!
I once did, I suppose,
But that was many years back down the line.

You try to kid yourself that there's a point
But deep inside you know it isn't so:
You've still got forty years of shit to go
And all a fucking total waste of time!

(1997)

At Writtle, in August

This is the time of year I'd like to die:
When the names on the war memorial make me cry;
When I'm really a part of the never-ending sky.
This is the time of year I'd like to die.

This is the time of year I want to die:
When my eyes are wet and my worried throat is dry;
When there's no-one to dictate my moves but I.
This is the time of year I want to die.

This is the time of year that I shall die:
When I'm free from the world and its ever-watchful eye;
When I'm all alone and I have no alibi.
This is the time of year that I shall die.

*   *   *

This is the time of year that Ian died:
When his relatives and friends were mortified;
When he was happy, even though they cried.
This is the time of year that Ian died.

(1998)

Essex

You can keep your package holiday and your airport carousel
And your passport and malaria jabs and your incomplete hotel
And your funny foreign currency and the pungent local smell:
A holiday for me is spent in Essex.

In Southend, Clacton, Walton, we have great seaside resorts,
With sandy, sun-kissed beaches where all you need is shorts.
There's jet-skiing and windsurfing and other watersports.
I reject your claim you can't find these in Essex.

You prefer quaint fishing villages? We've got those here as well:
From Brightlingsea to Leigh-on-Sea, from Burnham to Bradwell,
Where the fish is fresh as fish in Spain that you're so keen to sell.
I reject your claim you can't find these in Essex.

If you don't like sea and you want to be in the countryside instead,
You could retire to an open fire in a cottage near Thaxted,

For the countryside's so pretty here your eyes will leave your head.
I reject your claim you can't find this in Essex.

If you like your woodland, we have here some major forests stretching
From Highwoods up near Colchester to the great forest at Epping,
Or the Norman chase at Hatfield with its open, copsey setting.
I reject your claim you can't find this in Essex.

If its heritage that turns you on you've only got to go
To Rochford, Rayleigh, Colchester, to Dedham or Dunmow,
Or a hundred unspoilt villages that you do not even know.
I reject your claim you can't find this in Essex.

If you don't like being with people and you want to get away
Then go into the marshlands and pass a pleasant day
Rejoicing in your solitude where the sheep and birds hold sway.
I reject your claim you can't find peace in Essex.

So next time when you pressure me to buckle and conform

And I tell you I've no reason to comply with what's the norm

I hope you'll understand some more of where I'm coming from:

I've everything I want right here in Essex.

(2005)

In Fryerning Churchyard

The torment of my soul is eased a little as I close
The lychgate of the church at Fryerning
And enter in the garden where my relatives repose
And share the peace that they are breathing in.

The hills of Billericay and the fields across the road
Give welcome reassurance to my mind
As I pass by the fir trees of that friendly last abode
With which the paths and hedgerows there are lined.

I find a kind of peace in Fryerning churchyard which atones
For all the usual struggles in my life
And feel myself relax among the dead who made my bones
And offer me a haven from my strife.

Each gravestone of an ancestor calls out for me to pause
And pay respects to those who lie within.
I envy them their silence and the peace which reassures
And yearn to share the world that they are in.

When visiting is over I contrive a small detour,
So stringing out my stay before I go,
And muse upon the plots marked out on as yet unused lawn
Where one day I myself will lie below.

For when the nightmare's over and the constant calls to please
Can be no longer heard and are no more,
I'll pay one final visit with my mind at last at ease
And rest there with my friends in Plot H4.

With these thoughts in my head I heave a heavy final sigh,
My mind refreshed and once more feeling strong.
My spirits and my sanity restored I say goodbye,
Am able once again to soldier on.

The torment of my soul is eased a little as I close
The gate and leave the haven undisturbed,
Expectant of the day I'll share my relatives' repose
And no more have to battle with the world.

(2005)

Prelude to the Battle of Ashingdon (1016): The Danish Camp

The low sun shone upon the English shields
Aligned along the ridge at Ashingdon.
Canute could see some soldiers dashing down
The hillside, swift into the flattening fields.

Darkness departed, dawning day now came.
Canute's troops moved and pounding feet
Resounded round the valley where would meet
The English and the Danes. All took their aim

And arrows flew, foreshadowing ground attack
As soldiers swarmed from hills into the flat,
An unshown traitor yet to shape combat
And yet to let Canute push Edmund back.

'The English,' sneered Canute, 'defend their lands,
But know not yet they play into my hands.'

(2006)

Stop Pretending

Please stop pretending it will be alright
As she slips gentle into that good night.
She fought for life and now her fight is ending,
The end to all my tenderness and tending,
The end to my attempts to make things right.

My prayers unheard, my broken heart is rending,
Her broken, lifeless body isn't mending.
The tears of loss well up and cloud my sight.
She will not wake: her spirit's taken flight.
For those who think their love's life's neverending:

Stop pretending.

(2006)

Printed in the United Kingdom
by Lightning Source UK Ltd.
113500UKS00001B/106-129